MASTERING THE ART OF STOCK MARKET INVESTING

STRATEGIES FOR LONG-TERM SUCCESS

(A BEGINNER'S GUIDE)

Charles Lewis

Mastering The Art Of Stock Market Investing

Copyright© Charles Lewis 2023

All Rights Reserved

Mastering The Art Of Stock Market Investing

Mastering The Art Of Stock Market Investing

CHAPTER ONE

INTRODUCTION

CHAPTER TWO

UNDERSTANDING THE STOCK MARKET
HISTORY OF STOCK MARKETS

CHAPTER THREE

DEVELOPING A STOCK MARKET STRATEGY
SETTING INVESTMENT GOALS
RESEARCHING AND SELECTING STOCKS

CHAPTER FOUR

STOCK ANALYSIS TOOLS MARKET
FUNDAMENTAL ANALYSIS
TECHNICAL ANALYSIS
MARKET TRENDS AND INDICATORS
PORTFOLIO MANAGEMENT

CHAPTER FIVE

MAKING STOCK MARKET INVESTMENT
OPENING A BROKERAGE ACCOUNT
PLACING BUY AND SELL ORDERS
MONITORING AND MANAGING INVESTMENTS

CHAPTER SIX

STOCK MARKET RISKS AND CHALLENGES

Mastering The Art Of Stock Market Investing

MARKET VOLATILITY
ECONOMIC AND POLITICAL FACTORS AFFECTING THE STOCK MARKET.
PROTECTING AGAINST LOSS IN THE STOCK MARKET

CHAPTER SEVEN

ADVANCED STOCK MARKET STRATEGIS
SHORT SELLING
OPTION TRADING
DIVERSIFICATION AND ASSET ALLOCATION

CHAPTER EIGHT

CONCLUSION

Mastering The Art Of Stock Market Investing

Mastering The Art Of Stock Market Investing

CHAPTER ONE

INTRODUCTION

Welcome to "Navigating the Stock Market: Tips for Successful Investing"! Whether you are a seasoned investor or just starting out, understanding the stock market is essential for building wealth over the long term. In this guide, we will cover the fundamentals of the stock market and provide you with the tools and strategies you need to make informed investment decisions. We will explore different types of stocks, the role of stock exchanges, and how to conduct thorough market analysis. We will also discuss the risks and challenges of stock market investing and how to protect against loss. Finally, we will delve into more advanced strategies for maximizing your investment potential. By the end of this guide, you will have a solid foundation in the principles of stock market investing and the confidence to build a portfolio that aligns with your financial goals.

Chapter 1: Understanding the Stock Market

In this chapter, we will delve into the basics of the stock market and the various types of stocks that are available for investment. We will also discuss the role of stock exchanges and how they facilitate the buying and selling of stocks. By the end of this chapter, you will have a foundational understanding of the stock market and the different options available for investment.

Chapter 2: Developing a Stock Market Strategy

In this chapter, we will focus on the importance of setting investment goals and determining your risk tolerance. We will also discuss the importance of thorough research and how to select the right stocks for your portfolio. By the end of this chapter, you will have a clear strategy in place for navigating the stock market and maximizing your investment potential.

Chapter 3: Stock Market Analysis Tools

In this chapter, we will delve into the various tools and techniques used for stock market analysis, including fundamental analysis and technical analysis. We will also discuss market trends and indicators that can provide valuable insights into the performance of stocks. By the end of this chapter, you will be equipped with the knowledge and skills to conduct thorough market analysis and make informed investment decisions.

Chapter 4: Portfolio Management

In this chapter, we will be focusing on the importance of portfolio management and how to effectively manage and rebalance your portfolio. Proper portfolio management is essential for maximizing returns and minimizing risk in the stock market, and it's an important part of the investment process.

Chapter 5: Making Stock Market Investments

In this chapter, we will cover the steps for making stock market investments, including opening a brokerage account and placing buy and sell orders. We will also discuss the importance of monitoring and managing your investments to ensure long-term success. By the end of this chapter, you will have the knowledge and confidence to make your first stock market investments.

Chapter 6: Stock Market Risks and Challenges

In this chapter, we will delve into the risks and challenges of stock market investing, including market volatility, economic and political factors, and protecting against loss. We will also discuss strategies for managing risk and minimizing potential losses. By the end of this chapter, you will be equipped with the knowledge and tools to navigate the inherent risks of stock market investing.

Chapter 7: Advanced Stock Market Strategies

Mastering The Art Of Stock Market Investing

In this final chapter, we will delve into more advanced stock market strategies, including short selling, options trading, and diversification and asset allocation. We will discuss the pros and cons of each strategy and provide guidance on how to incorporate them into your investment portfolio. By the end of this chapter, you will have a deeper understanding of the various tools and techniques available for maximizing your investment potential.

CHAPTER TWO
UNDERSTANDING THE STOCK MARKET

What is the stock market? Simply put, the stock market is a place where publicly traded companies sell shares of their stock to investors. These investors become part owners of the company and are entitled to a share of the profits. The stock market is an essential component of the global financial system and is often used as a barometer for the overall health of the economy.

HISTORY OF STOCK MARKETS

Antwerp is home to the oldest stock exchange in the world. However, it is thought that the Amsterdam Stock Exchange (ASE), founded in 1602 by the Dutch East India Company, is responsible for the widespread acceptance of stock trading. The transcontinental spice trade between Europe and Asia played a significant role in its development.

One method by which trading companies could mitigate the risk of perilous voyages that could cause sizable financial losses as well as human casualties was the issuance of equity. A successful expedition could bring about fantastic profits and riches for stockholders. In today's terms, the Dutch East India Company was worth $7.9 trillion at its height.

Mastering The Art Of Stock Market Investing

As a point of reference, Apple, the market's richest company, recently passed the $2 trillion threshold. The London Stock Exchange rose to become the largest stock market in the world by the nineteenth century as a result of the British East India Company's success in maritime trading. However, American exchanges were the focus of the twentieth century. A casual group of traders started the NYSE by exchanging shares at a coffee shop in Lower Manhattan.

More than 200 years after its official inauguration, it had grown to be the largest exchange in the world. It served as the nation's primary stock market listing location for nearly 200 years. Entrepreneurs now have yet another significant choice thanks to the 1971 launch of NASDAQ. The NASDAQ is more heavily weighted in the technology sector than the NYSE, which tends to favor more established industries.

India's Bombay Stock Exchange is home to Asia's oldest stock exchange. In 1875, it first began. It is not, however, the biggest. Its volume has been surpassed by the more recent Shanghai Stock Exchange, which was founded in 1990. Early on, stock trading was viewed as a risky form of gambling and was stigmatized. The stock market has changed, and it now serves as a tool for creating and accumulating wealth thanks to the development of scientific techniques to analyze price changes and individual stocks as well as sophisticated modeling.

Disclosures are now required, and businesses are required to submit quarterly earnings reports that include specifics about their costs and borrowings. Companies that defraud inexperienced investors are prosecuted by organizations like the Securities Exchange Commission (SEC), which regulates the markets.

Types of stocks and their characteristics

There are two main categories of stocks: common stock and preferred stock. Common stock represents ownership in a company and gives shareholders the right to vote on certain matters, such as the election of board members. Preferred stock, on the other hand, typically does not have voting rights but may have a higher claim on the company's assets and earnings.

In addition to common and preferred stock, there are also various types of stocks based on the size and sector of the company. For example, small-cap stocks represent smaller companies that have a market capitalization of less than $2 billion. Mid-cap stocks represent companies with a market capitalization between $2 billion and $10 billion, while large-cap stocks represent companies with a market capitalization of more than $10 billion. There are also sector-specific stocks, such as technology stocks or healthcare stocks, which focus on a specific industry.

There are additional stock categories that merit discussing in the context of addiction. For instance, growth stocks are equities of businesses that analysts predict will expand more quickly than the market as a whole. These businesses may not have a good history of paying dividends, but they have the potential to experience tremendous capital growth. Value stocks, on the other hand, are examples of businesses that are now trading for less than they are truly worth. These equities could have lower volatility than growth stocks and a higher dividend yield.

Market capitalization, or the entire worth of a company's outstanding shares of stock, is another crucial notion to comprehend. To calculate this, multiply the number of outstanding shares by the price per share on the open market. Stocks are frequently divided into small-cap, mid-cap, and large-cap categories based on market capitalization.

There are more stock categories besides ordinary and preferred shares that are noteworthy. For instance, penny stocks are shares of stock that are normally sold at a price of less than $5 per share. These stocks have a high level of risk and are frequently connected to small, extremely speculative businesses. Because of this, penny stocks are not appropriate for all investors, and you should do your homework before investing.

Market liquidity, or the capacity to purchase and sell a stock rapidly and at a consistent price, is another crucial idea to comprehend. Stocks with high liquidity are simpler to purchase and sell, and their prices tend to be more stable; by contrast, stocks with low liquidity may be more challenging to trade, and their price fluctuations may be more pronounced. When selecting companies for your portfolio, market liquidity is crucial to take into account as it can effect how easy and expensive it is to acquire and sell equities.

In addition to common and preferred stock, there are also other types of securities that are worth mentioning. For example, bonds are debt securities that represent loans made by investors to companies or governments. Bonds typically pay periodic interest payments to investors and return the principal at maturity. Bond prices are influenced by factors such as the creditworthiness of the issuer, the prevailing interest rate environment, and the term of the bond.

Another important concept to understand is market indexing, which is a way of measuring the performance of a group of stocks. Market indexes, such as the S&P 500 or the Dow Jones Industrial Average, are used as benchmarks for the overall stock market and are often used to track the performance of mutual funds and other investment vehicles. Market indexing can be a useful tool for investors looking to gain broad exposure to the stock market without the need to buy and sell individual stocks.

The role of stock exchanges

These are platforms where buyers and sellers can come together to trade stocks. The two most well-known stock exchanges are the New York Stock Exchange (NYSE) and the NASDAQ. These exchanges have strict listing requirements and are highly regulated, ensuring that only reputable companies can trade on their platforms.

It's also worth noting that stocks can be traded on different exchanges around the world. For example, a company may be listed on the NYSE in the United States but also have shares traded on the London Stock Exchange or the Tokyo Stock Exchange. This global reach of the stock market allows investors to diversify their portfolio and potentially tap into growth opportunities in different regions.

Additionally, it's important to keep in mind that stocks can be traded in a variety of formats, including physical certificates and electronic holdings. Physical certificates, often called "paper stock," are written records that show a person has stock in a corporation. Whenever the stock is purchased or sold, these certificates must be transferred and registered in the shareholder's name. On the other hand, electronic holdings signify ownership in a corporation and are electronically recorded in a brokerage account. These investments are becoming increasingly common and provide the convenience of online stock trading.

It's also important to keep in mind that the stock market is always changing as new businesses enter the market and older ones experience various stages of expansion and decline. In order to make sure that your investment portfolio is in line with your financial objectives and risk tolerance, it's crucial to examine and update it on a regular basis. This could entail rebalancing your portfolio, adding or selling equities, or changing your asset allocation. It's also important to remember that numerous rules and oversight organizations exist to guarantee fairness and openness in the stock market. For instance, the U.S. Securities and Exchange Commission (SEC) is in charge of policing federal securities laws and overseeing the stock market. The SEC mandates publicly traded corporations to disclose financial and other information to shareholders in order to safeguard investors from deceptive and manipulative tactics.

- Securities Listing: A variety of securities, including equities (such as common stock), debt (such as corporate bonds), structured products (such as exchange-traded funds, or ETFs), and options, are listed on an exchange. Companies list on Nasdaq to provide themselves with the chance to raise funds through public ownership, and their shares of stock turn into securities as a result. To list (and remain listed) on the exchange, each form of security must adhere to a certain set of listing rules.
- Membership: A broker will execute a trade on the exchange by submitting a quote into the system when an investor submits an order to buy or sell a security. Brokers must be members of the exchange in order to access the exchange systems. Every part of member firms' trading is governed by regulations. They

must, among other things, have documented processes to prevent any actions that might be detrimental to investors and be adequately financed (i.e., have a sizable fund available for deployment).
- Monitoring: Excluding options, the daily average volume of shares traded on Nasdaq marketplaces is around 1.9 billion. The execution of each of these trades is tracked to make sure that fair prices are being used. The exchange's surveillance teams use real-time surveillance technology to do this.
- The surveillance technology searches for trades that don't appear to be in line with prices that have already been set. If the price is sufficiently different from the current market price, the trade can be canceled or "broken." The surveillance team keeps an eye out for information that could cause a sharp drop in the stock price of the company, and it has the power to halt trade if necessary (for example, if a car company announces a recall of their vehicles or if a company files for bankruptcy).
- Enforcement: Unlike the enforcement of regulations for listed businesses, the exchange's own enforcement team is in

charge of looking into violations of the rules by member firms or other market players and assessing whether fees or other penalties are warranted.

- The Future of the Exchange: Exchange regulation must develop as markets and technologies advance to effectively safeguard investors. To accomplish this, exchanges must consider how to make use of the technology that exists today and examine trends to get ready to make use of the technology that will exist in the future. Technologies like artificial intelligence (AI) are already in use at Nasdaq.

CHAPTER THREE
DEVELOPING A STOCK MARKET STRATEGY
SETTING INVESTMENT GOALS

"Investing in knowledge yields the finest returns."
[Benjamin Franklin]

First and foremost, it's important to have a clear understanding of your financial goals and how the stock market fits into your overall financial plan. Are you looking to generate income, build wealth over the long term, or achieve a combination of both? Understanding your goals will help guide your investment decisions and ensure that your portfolio aligns with your financial objectives.

Another important factor to consider when selecting stocks for your portfolio is the investment horizon. This refers to the length of time that you plan to hold the stock. If you have a long-term investment horizon, you may be more willing to take on higher levels of risk in exchange for the potential for higher returns. On the other hand, if you have a shorter investment horizon, you may be more focused on preserving capital and may opt for lower-risk investments with more stable returns.

Your investment timeline is a crucial issue to take into account when making stock market investments. This can help you make better financial choices because it refers to how long you intend to hold your investments. For instance, if you plan to make investments over a long period of time, you may be more willing to accept greater levels of risk in exchange for the possibility of greater returns. On the other side, if your investing horizon is shorter, you might be more concerned with capital preservation and choose less risky products with more consistent returns. It's also worth mentioning that there are various investment vehicles available to help you invest in the stock market, such as mutual funds, exchange-traded funds (ETFs), and index funds. These vehicles offer the convenience of being able to invest in a diversified portfolio of stocks without the need to buy and sell individual stocks. However, it's important to carefully research and compare these investment vehicles to ensure that they align with your investment goals and risk tolerance.

1.Goals: Think about your motivations for investing.

Money-making is an aim of investments, but there are other factors at play as well. What will you do with this cash? You should be ready for a mid- to long-term commitment, often lasting at least five years, if it's for purposes like as making up an income deficit, retirement planning, paying off existing debts, or purchasing another asset. If your goal is to get rich before then, saving might be a better option.

2. Risk: Take into account your level of risk tolerance.

Your investment's value may increase or decrease, and in the end, your investment goals and objectives will depend on how comfortable you are taking risks. Consider where you can take risks and where you can't, while keeping in mind your other financial obligations. For instance, if you're getting close to retirement, you'll want to steer clear of any significant losses right before you withdraw your funds.

3. Determine the length of time you want to invest.

Generally speaking, the longer your money is invested, the greater the chance that it will increase in value and help you achieve your goal. However, how long you invest will depend on the results you hope to achieve. Anything you'll need money for in the next five years or less is typically seen as short-term, whereas goals outlined over the next five to ten years are regarded as mid-term. Long-term objectives often span time frames of more than ten years.

4. Make a plan for your investments.

Mastering The Art Of Stock Market Investing

You need to find any appropriate investment options when you are clear on your objectives and goals and after you have thought about how much risk and time you can accept. In general, it's advisable to begin with a low-risk investment, such as cash ISAs. Unit trusts and other medium-risk investments could be included if you're willing to tolerate increased volatility. You won't be prepared for something with a higher level of risk unless you've amassed several low- and medium-risk investments.

5. Be creative and create a varied portfolio.

Making a balanced, diversified investment portfolio is one of the best strategies to guard against the market's ups and downs. The economy, interest rates, politics, wars, and even the weather can all have an impact on an investment. What's good for one investment could be bad for another, so when one does well, another might underperform. Therefore, investing all of your money in one type of investment is a dangerous move.

Determining risk tolerance

The ability and willingness to withstand a drop in the value of your investments is known as risk tolerance. When trying to gauge your level of risk tolerance, consider how at ease you will feel holding onto your positions through sharp falls in the stock market.

Mastering The Art Of Stock Market Investing

It's essential to consider your risk tolerance when investing in the stock market. The stock market carries inherent risks, such as market volatility and economic and political factors. While these risks can't be completely eliminated, they can be managed through proper asset allocation and diversification. It's important to determine your risk tolerance and choose investments that align with your comfort level. This may involve taking on more risk for the potential for higher returns or opting for lower-risk investments with more stable returns.

It's also crucial to be aware of the costs and fees connected with stock market investment. This comprises commissions for trading, brokerage fees, and mutual fund costs. Over time, these fees can have a substantial impact on your profits, so it's crucial to pick a brokerage company and investment vehicle with reasonable expenses. Your total financial status is a key consideration when making stock market investments. This comprises your present earnings, costs, debt, and other financial commitments. It's crucial to assess your financial condition clearly and to confirm that you can afford the risks involved in stock market trading.

It's also important to keep in mind that a variety of external factors, like monetary circumstances, political developments, and world trends, can have an impact on the stock market. It's crucial to keep up with these elements and think about how they can affect your finances. To reduce the risk of any one investment or asset type underperforming, you might diversify your portfolio.

When making stock market investments, it's necessary to take professional advisers' roles—such as those of wealth managers or financial advisors—into account. These experts can help you manage the complexity of the stock market and offer insightful advice on investment ideas. However, it's crucial to pick a qualified advisor who is knowledgeable, trustworthy, and compatible with your financial objectives and risk tolerance.

1. What are your goals for your investments? Do you frequently make investments with the goal of increasing the value of your nest egg? Or if you currently have a respectable nest egg and are aiming to protect it and live off the income it generates rather than growing it? Each will indicate a different level of tolerance for price risk on the downside.

2. When is the money needed? An important factor in the equation is your time horizon. The lower your risk tolerance, the sooner you need the money. The amount of money you're saving for retirement, which won't be needed for many more years, has a

completely different time horizon than the amount you'll need for a down payment on a house next year.

3. How would you respond if this year your portfolio lost 20% of its value? You must consider potential difficulties and worst-case scenarios while evaluating your risk tolerance. Would you scream at the top of your lungs and withdraw all of your money if your investment lost 20% of its value? Or otherwise, would you keep the money invested and think about investing more to take advantage of the bargain?

RESEARCHING AND SELECTING STOCKS

Researching and choosing stocks for your portfolio should begin once you have a firm grasp on your financial objectives and risk tolerance. This entails conducting in-depth research on potential investments, which includes examining the financial accounts of the business, evaluating its management team, and examining its position in the market. To lower risk and boost possible profits, it's crucial to diversify your portfolio by investing in a range of other businesses and industries.

It is important to remember that no investment strategy is perfect and that there are inherent hazards in the stock market that cannot be totally eradicated. These risks must be understood and effectively managed through appropriate diversification and asset allocation. It's also a good idea to check your portfolio on a regular basis to make sure it's in line with your financial objectives and risk tolerance.

The stock market is a long-term investment, and while it can be volatile in the short term, it is crucial to keep this in mind. It's critical to keep a long-term perspective and not let momentary market changes make you reconsider your investing plan. You may improve your chances of making money in the stock market by staying the course and adhering to your investment strategy.

How To Research stock

Researching stocks is similar to looking for a car. You can make a decision based only on technical specifications, but it's also crucial to take into account the ride quality, the manufacturer's reputation, and whether the interior color will hide dog hair.

Fundamental analysis is the term used by investors to describe this kind of stock study.

When learning how to research stocks, you should consider a variety of elements to analyze a stock and determine whether it merits a place in your portfolio, including the company's financials, leadership team, and competitors.

Before we get started, it's important to keep in mind that stocks are long-term investments because they are quite risky; you need time to ride out any ups and downs and reap the rewards of long-term gains. For money you won't need for at least the next five years, investing in equities is the best option.

1. Compile your stock research resources

Start by going over the business's finances. Gathering the following documents, which businesses must submit to the U.S. Securities and Exchange Commission (SEC), is the first step in quantitative research

Best websites for stock research

A searchable database of the aforementioned forms is available on the Electronic Data Gathering, Analysis, and Retrieval (EDGAR) website of the SEC. It's a useful tool for discovering how to investigate stocks.

2. Focus more intently

These financial reports are filled with a ton of numbers, making it easy to become overwhelmed.

Focus on the following line items to learn about the quantifiable internal workings of a company:

- Revenue: The amount of money a business earned within the given time period. Because it appears first on the revenue statement, it is frequently referred to as the "top line." Revenue is occasionally divided into "operating revenue" and "nonoperating revenue." Because it comes from the company's main line of business, operating revenue is the most revealing. One-time business activities, like selling an asset, are a common source of non-operating revenue.
- Net income: This is the total amount of money a firm has generated after operating costs, taxes, and depreciation are removed from revenue. It is referred to as the "bottom line" since it is presented at the end of the income statement. Your gross compensation is equivalent to revenue, and your net income is the amount that is left over after paying your taxes and living expenses.
- Earnings and Earnings per share (EPS) Earnings per share are calculated by dividing earnings by the total number of trading shares. This figure displays a company's profitability on a per-share basis, which facilitates comparisons

with other businesses. The "trailing twelve months" is referred to when earnings per share are followed by "(ttm)." Earnings are not a great financial indicator because they do not reveal how effectively the company uses its capital. Some businesses decide to reinvest their earnings back into the company. Others disburse them as dividends to shareholders.

- Price-earnings ratio (P/E): You may calculate a company's trailing P/E ratio by dividing its current stock price by its earnings per share, which are typically over the past 12 months. You may calculate the forward P/E by dividing the company's price by the estimated earnings predicted by Wall Street experts. By using this metric, you can determine how much investors are prepared to pay in order to receive $1 in current earnings from a company. Remember that analyst projections are infamously short-term oriented and that the P/E ratio is derived from the potentially inaccurate assessment of earnings per share. It is therefore not a valid stand-alone metric.
- Return on assets (ROA) and return on equity (ROE) A company's return on equity, expressed as a percentage, shows how much profit it makes off of each dollar its shareholders have contributed. The equity is

owned by the shareholders. Return on assets reveals what portion of earnings a company makes from each dollar of assets. Each is obtained by dividing the annual net income of the company by a particular metric. The efficiency with which the company generates profits is also indicated by these percentages. Again, be on the lookout for gotchas. By repurchasing shares to lower the shareholder equity denominator, a corporation can artificially increase its return on equity. In the same vein, increasing debt increases the number of assets utilized to determine the return on assets, such as loans to finance property or increase inventory.

3. Use qualitative stock analysis.

Qualitative stock research offers the technicolor details that give you a more accurate image of a company's operations and future, whereas quantitative stock research discloses the black-and-white financials of a company's tale.

"Buy into a firm because you want to own it, not because you want the stock to go up," famously said Warren Buffett. This is due to the fact that when you buy stocks, you make a personal investment in a company.

You can use the following queries to help you weed out possible business partners:

- How does the business generate revenue? When it comes to a retailer whose primary activity is selling clothing, that can be quite clear. Sometimes it's not, as in the case of a fast-food chain that makes the majority of its money through franchising deals or an electronics company that depends on consumer financing for expansion. Investing in firms that make sense and that you actually understand is a sound strategy that has worked well for Buffett.
- Is there a competitive edge for this business? Look for a quality in the company that makes it challenging to duplicate, match, or surpass. This could be, among other things, its reputation, commercial strategy, capacity for innovation, research prowess, ownership of patents, operational competence, or superior distribution capacities. The strength of the competitive advantage increases with the difficulty of competitors breaching the company's moat.
- How effective is the management group? A firm is only as good as its leaders' ability to set the organization's direction. You can learn a

lot about management by reading the transcripts of company conference calls and annual reports. Do some research on the board of directors of the business, who sit in the boardroom as the shareholders' representatives. Be aware of boards that are primarily made up of business insiders. You want to see a good mix of independent thinkers who can evaluate management's activities with objectivity.

- What might possibly fail? We're not discussing events that can have a short-term impact on the stock price of the company but rather fundamental shifts that have a long-term impact on a company's capacity for expansion. Use hypothetical "what if" situations to spot potential red flags. A significant patent expires, the CEO's replacement steers the company in a different direction, a strong rival enters the market, or new technology usurps the company's goods or services.

4. Set the context for your stock study.

As you can see, there are an almost limitless number of measures and ratios that investors may use to evaluate a company's overall financial health and determine the intrinsic value of its stock. However, focusing simply on a business's earnings or sales from a single year or the management team's most recent actions results in an inaccurate image.

Build a thorough narrative about the business and the aspects that make it deserving of a long-term relationship before investing in any stock. Context is crucial in doing this.

Pull back your research's focus to consider historical data for a long-term context. This will help you gain understanding of the company's ability to persevere through difficult times, respond to obstacles, and enhance its performance over time while generating value for shareholders.

Examine the company's position in relation to the overall picture by contrasting the data and key ratios with industry averages and other businesses in a related or identical industry. Research resources are readily available through brokers' websites. Utilizing your broker's educational resources, such as a stock screener, is the simplest approach to make these comparisons.

Mastering The Art Of Stock Market Investing

CHAPTER FOUR
STOCK ANALYSIS TOOLS MARKET

In this chapter, we will be focusing on the various tools and techniques used for stock market analysis. This is an essential step in the investment process, as it helps investors make informed decisions and identify potential opportunities in the stock market

One of the most common tools used for stock market analysis is fundamental analysis. This involves evaluating a company's financial statements and other fundamental data to determine its intrinsic value and potential for future growth. This may include reviewing the company's revenue, earnings, debt, and other financial metrics to determine its financial health and stability.

Another important tool for stock market analysis is technical analysis, which involves using historical price and volume data to identify patterns and trends in the market. Technical analysts may use various charting techniques, such as trend lines and moving averages, to identify buying and selling opportunities in the stock market.

It's also worth mentioning that the stock market is influenced by a wide range of external factors, such as economic conditions, political events, and global trends. It's important to stay informed about these factors and to consider how they may impact your investments. This may involve diversifying your portfolio to mitigate the risk of any one investment or asset class underperforming.

Industry analysis, which examines the trends and dynamics of a specific industry or area, is another technique for stock market analysis. Investors can use this to find businesses that are well-positioned to take advantage of industry-specific trends and opportunities.

Investors can also seek out the counsel and insights of financial planners, wealth managers, and other qualified consultants in addition to these instruments. These experts can help investors manage the complexity of the stock market and offer invaluable advice on investment ideas. However, it's crucial to pick a qualified advisor who is knowledgeable, trustworthy, and compatible with your financial objectives and risk tolerance.

Last but not least, it's important to note that no investment strategy is infallible and that there are inherent hazards in the stock market that cannot be totally eradicated. These risks must be understood and effectively managed through appropriate diversification and asset allocation. It's also a good idea to check your portfolio on a regular basis to make sure it's in line with your financial objectives and risk tolerance.

The fact that investors can combine fundamental, technical, and industry analysis to make wise investment selections should also be noted. This could entail looking over a company's financial accounts and other important information, examining previous price and volume statistics, and researching market trends and dynamics. Investors can get a more thorough grasp of a company's potential and make more educated investment decisions by employing a holistic approach to stock market analysis.

The importance of market sentiment should be taken into account while employing these tools and strategies for stock market analysis. This speaks to the general attitude or view of the market and is influenced by a variety of elements, including monetary conditions, political developments, and world trends. Market mood should be taken into account when making investment decisions because it may have a big impact on both the performance of certain stocks and the market as a whole.

FUNDAMENTAL ANALYSIS

An experienced investor who has made a variety of investments, including stock investments, will tell you that fundamental and technical research are the cornerstones of stock investment analysis. In-depth research of the company that issues the stock you want to trade or invest in is the major focus of fundamental analysis in stock investment analysis. Therefore, fundamental analysis entails evaluating stocks using financial, quantitative, and qualitative components that help you ascertain the inherent worth of a company. Just to be sure you are on the right road and can distinguish between technical analysis and fundamental analysis, you should be aware that technical analysis involves tactics that heavily rely on the price movement of a particular company. The majority of technical analysis assesses if a stock's present trend will continue, and if there is any indication that it won't, the timing of its reversal is also evaluated.

Fundamental Analysis at Its Core

How do you examine a company's fundamentals? Fundamental analysis is one of the most fruitful types of analysis in the history of the stock market. In some manner, every analysis requires looking at securities. It is believed that both macroeconomic and microeconomic factors have the power to affect a security's value. These are factors that are influenced by the state of the market, the state of the economy, the state of the finances, and the management skills of the organization. The assessment of any security's intrinsic value serves as the main driving force behind a fundamental examination. Then, this needs to be contrasted with the current stock price. This will allow you to determine whether a security is overvalued or undervalued.

Here's how to conduct stock research like a true market pro.

1. Examining Financial Statements: Share market analysis is primarily a mathematical exercise. The financial accounts of the company should be your first port of call if you already know which one you want to invest in. These claims are available to the general public. The company's performance can be summed up in unbiased terms by quickly reading through the balance sheet, income statement, and cash flow statement. Financial statements provide data on sales, profit margins, and the potential for future profitability, all of which can be used to assess the company's earning potential in the future.

2. Industry Analysis: Comparing a company's performance to that of its rivals or other businesses in the same sector might shed more light on how well it is doing in terms of industry norms. Resources that aid in assembling a clear picture of industry

trends include trade journals, research papers, surveys, and annual reports released by the company.

3. Researching Stocks: One must look at the company's valuation to determine whether a stock is worth the price it is currently trading at. Stock prices should be impacted by a company's earnings, but other variables, such as a worldwide health crisis, foreign investment, or a change in legislation, might disproportionately increase or decrease a stock's value. A stock's price-to-earnings (P/E) ratio is another useful tool for determining whether the stock's price is excessive in relation to its earnings per share. Analysts often examine historical data, focusing on earnings per share over time. A high P/E ratio could be a sign that a stock is overvalued, while a low number could be a sign that a firm is undervalued. It is one of the criteria used to assess if a stock is one that should be purchased.

4. Price Targets: Finding a price target is the main goal of all stock research and analysis. Stock analysts forecast a stock's future price based on the aforementioned parameters. Your entry into or departure from the investment is determined by the price target. The price objective is not a fixed amount and is affected by market forces, fresh information, and developments throughout the

world. However, it is the most reliable way to determine whether buying a company at its current market value now would allow you to profit from it in the future.

TECHNICAL ANALYSIS

By examining statistical trends gleaned from trading activity, such as price movement and volume, technical analysis is a trading discipline used to assess investments and pinpoint trading opportunities. Technical analysis focuses on the analysis of price and volume as opposed to fundamental analysis, which seeks to determine the value of an asset based on financial outcomes like sales and earnings.

Key Lessons

1. The trading discipline of technical analysis is used to assess investments and find trading opportunities in price movements and patterns visible on charts.

2. According to technical analysts, a security's previous trading activity and price changes might be useful predictors of the security's future price moves.

3. Fundamental analysis, which emphasizes a company's financials rather than past price trends or

stock trends, can be contrasted with technical analysis.

By Means Of Technical Analysis.

Technical analysis is frequently used with other types of research by analysts in the industry. Retail traders may base their choices only on a security's price charts and comparable data, but in practice, equity analysts rarely confine their inquiry to just fundamental or technical analysis.

Any security with previous trading data might be subject to technical analysis. This covers securities such as stocks, futures, commodities, fixed-income securities, currencies, and others. Technical analysis, which focuses on short-term price changes, is really much more common in the commodities and currency markets.

Stocks, bonds, futures, currency pairs, and nearly any other tradable asset that is often influenced by forces of supply and demand are all vulnerable to technical analysis' attempts to forecast price movement. Some people actually think that technical analysis is only the study of supply and demand forces as they manifest themselves in market price changes for a security.

Although price fluctuations are the most typical subject of technical analysis, some analysts also keep watch over other metrics like trade volume or open interest levels.

Comparison between technical and fundamental analysis

When it comes to how to approach the markets, the two main schools of thought, fundamental analysis and technical analysis, are at different ends of the spectrum. Like every investment technique or philosophy, both methodologies have their proponents and detractors. They are both used to investigate and predict future patterns in stock values.

By attempting to calculate a stock's intrinsic worth, fundamental analysis is a technique for assessing equities. Fundamental analysts research everything, including corporate management, the state of the economy as a whole, and market circumstances. Fundamental analysts pay close attention to factors including earnings, expenses, assets, and liabilities.

Technical analysis differs from fundamental analysis in that the only inputs are the stock's price and volume. The fundamental presumption is that price already takes into account all known fundamentals; hence, it is unnecessary to pay close attention to

Mastering The Art Of Stock Market Investing

them. Instead of attempting to determine a security's fundamental value, technical analysts analyze stock charts to spot patterns and trends that portend what will happen to a stock in the future.

MARKET TRENDS AND INDICATORS

It's also important to note that a wide range of outside influences, including monetary circumstances, political developments, and world trends, have an impact on the stock market. It's crucial to keep up with these elements and think about how they can affect your finances. To reduce the risk of any one investment or asset type underperforming, you might diversify your portfolio. It's important to note that no investment strategy is infallible and that there are inherent hazards in the stock market that cannot be totally eradicated. These risks must be understood and effectively managed through appropriate diversification and asset allocation. It's also a good idea to check your portfolio on a regular basis to make sure it's in line with your financial objectives and risk tolerance.

Market Indicators

Quantitative in nature, market indicators try to foretell market movements by interpreting stock or financial index data. Technical indicators have formulas and ratios, and market indicators are a subset of those. They support investors' trading and investment decisions.

Points To Note

- Market indicators have a quantitative aspect and evaluate stock or financial index data in an effort to predict market movements.
- Market indicators, a class of technical indicators, are frequently made up of formulas and ratios.
- Market sentiment, advance-decline, and moving averages are a few of the commonly used market indicators.

Knowledge of Market Indicators

In order to arrive at a conclusion, market indicators and technical indicators both apply a statistical formula to a set of data points. The distinction is that market indicators draw their data from a variety of securities as opposed to just one. Market indicators frequently appear on their own chart rather than above or below an index price chart.

The majority of stock market indicators are developed by examining the market breadth, or the ratio of businesses making new highs to new lows, as it indicates the direction of the general trend.

The following are the top two categories of market indicators:

Indicators of market breadth measure how many stocks are going in the same direction as a bigger trend. The advance-decline line, for instance, compares the quantity of advancing stocks to the quantity of decreasing stocks.

Using price and volume comparisons, market sentiment indicators can tell if investors are bullish or bearish on the market as a whole. For instance, the put-call ratio considers the quantity of put options as compared to call options over a specific time period.

Market Trends

The general course of a market or the value of an asset is referred to as a "trend." Trendlines or price action that show when the price is making higher swing high points and higher swing low points for an uptrend or lower swing low points and lower swing peaks for a downtrend are used to identify trends in technical analysis.

Contrarian traders look for trend reversals or choose to trade the opposite of the trend, while many traders choose to trade in the same direction as a trend. Markets for stocks, bonds, and futures all experience uptrends and downtrends. The rise or decline of monthly economic statistics from month to month is an example of a trend in the data.

Main Takeaways

- The price of a market, an asset, or a statistic tends in one general direction.
- Rising data points, such as higher swing highs and lower swing lows, are indicators of uptrends.
- Data points that are falling, such as lower swing lows and lower swing highs, are indicators of downtrends.
- A lot of traders choose to trade in the trend's direction in an effort to profit from the trend's continuation.
- There are several methods that can be used to identify the trend and signal when it is about to reverse, including price action, trendlines, and technical indicators.

How to Use Trends

Different types of technical analysis, including trendlines, price action, and technical indicators, can be used by traders to spot trends. For instance, while the relative strength index (RSI) is intended to represent the strength of a trend at any particular period, trendlines may show the direction of a trend.

An overall price increase indicates an upswing. There will always be oscillations because nothing goes straight up for very long, but an uptrend only exists when the main tendency is higher. Recent swing lows and swing highs should be higher than earlier swing lows and highs, respectively. The uptrend may lose momentum or reverse into a decline once this structure begins to crumble. Lower swing lows and lower swing highs make up downtrends.

Until there is proof to the contrary, traders may believe the upward trend will last as long as it has. Such proof could come in the form of lower swing lows or highs, the price crossing below a trendline, or bearish technical indicators. Traders concentrate on buying while the trend is upward in an effort to profit from a sustained price increase.

When the trend shifts downward, traders put more emphasis on shorting or selling in an effort to reduce losses or benefit from the drop in price. Most (but not all) downtrends do end, so as the price drops, more traders start to see it as a deal and enter the market to buy. This can result in the return of an upward trend.

Investors that are primarily interested in fundamental analysis may also use trends. Changes in revenue, earnings, or other business or economic metrics are examined in this type of analysis. For instance, fundamental analysts would search for trends in sales growth and earnings per share. If earnings have increased over the previous four quarters, this is a promising development. But if earnings have fallen for the previous four quarters, that indicates a bad pattern.

A range or trendless period is when there is no discernible upward or downward movement across time, or when there is no trend at all.

Trendlines Utilized

Using trendlines, which join a string of highs (in a downtrend) or lows (in an uptrend), is a typical method of spotting trends. A sequence of higher lows is connected by an uptrend, providing a base for upcoming price movements. A sequence of lower highs is connected by downtrends, forming a barrier to further market movement. These trendlines exhibit both support and resistance as well as the general trend.

Although trendlines are effective in indicating general direction, they frequently need to be redrew. For instance, if the price falls below the trendline during an upswing, it doesn't necessarily signal the trend is gone. The price can drop below the trendline before resuming its upward movement. In such a situation, it might be necessary to redraft the trendline to account for the new price movement.

It is not recommended to only use trendlines to identify trends. To help determine if a trend is ending or not, the majority of specialists also frequently use price action and other technical indicators. A dip below the trendline in the aforementioned example isn't necessarily a sell signal, but it might be if the price also descends below a previous swing low and/or technical indicators are becoming negative.

PORTFOLIO MANAGEMENT

Proper portfolio management is essential for maximizing returns and minimizing risk in the stock market, and it's an important part of the investment process. Portfolio management is the process of choosing, prioritizing, and managing an organization's programs and projects in accordance with its strategic goals and ability to carry them out.

In order to maximize return on investment, it is important to strike a balance between implementing change initiatives and maintaining business as usual.

Mastering The Art Of Stock Market Investing

One of the key aspects of portfolio management is diversification. This involves investing in a variety of different assets and asset classes in order to reduce the risk of any one investment or asset class underperforming. By diversifying your portfolio, you can mitigate the impact of market volatility and increase your chances of success in the stock market.

Another important aspect of portfolio management is asset allocation. This involves determining the appropriate mix of stocks, bonds, and other assets based on your investment goals and risk tolerance. By properly allocating your assets, you can optimize your portfolio's potential for returns while minimizing risk.

The establishment of specific investing objectives is a crucial component of portfolio management. This entails choosing your financial goals and developing a strategy to reach them. Setting both short-term and long-term goals, such as saving for a down payment on a home or retirement planning, may be necessary. You can map out your portfolio and make educated investment choices that support your financial objectives by establishing defined investing goals.

Portfolio management includes monitoring and analyzing your portfolio on a regular basis, in addition to diversification and asset allocation. In order to maintain your portfolio's alignment with your financial goals and risk tolerance, this may entail monitoring the performance of your investments, keeping up with market trends and financial news, and making any modifications. it's important to note that no investment strategy is infallible and that there are inherent hazards in the stock market that cannot be totally eradicated. These risks must be understood and properly managed through asset allocation, diversification, and risk management techniques. Investors can successfully manage their money and raise their chances of success on the stock market by putting these portfolio management ideas into practice.

Portfolio management knowledge

While people have the option to create and manage their own portfolios, qualified professional portfolio managers act on behalf of clients. The ultimate objective of the portfolio manager is to maximize the projected return on the investments while maintaining a reasonable degree of risk exposure.

The capacity to evaluate opportunities, dangers, and threats across the complete spectrum of investments is necessary for portfolio management. Debt versus equity, domestic versus foreign, growth versus safety, and other trade-offs are among the options.

Types of Portfolio Management

- Active Portfolio Management

When using an active management strategy, investors try to exceed a certain index, such as the Standard & Poor's 500 Index or the Russell 1000 Index, by using fund managers or brokers to purchase and sell stocks.

An individual portfolio manager, co-managers, or a group of managers actively make investment choices on behalf of an actively managed investment fund. An actively managed fund's success is reliant on extensive analysis, market foresight, and the knowledge of the portfolio manager or management group.

Active portfolio managers closely monitor market movements, changes in the economy, developments in the political environment, and business-related news. In an effort to profit from anomalies, this data is utilized to time the purchase or sale of investments. Active managers assert that these procedures will increase the possibility of returns that are greater than those obtained by merely replicating the holdings on a specific index.

Attempting to outperform the market invariably increases market risk. This specific risk is eliminated by indexing because there is no chance of stock selection mistakes due to human error. Index funds have lower cost ratios and are more tax-efficient than actively managed funds since they are traded less frequently.

- Passive Portfolio Management

The objective of passive portfolio management, also known as index fund management, is to match the performance of a specific market index or benchmark. Using the same weighting that they reflect in the index, managers purchase the same stocks that are listed on the index.

A passively managed portfolio can be set up as a unit investment trust, mutual fund, or exchange-traded fund (ETF). Because each index fund has a portfolio manager whose role is to replicate the index rather than choose the assets bought or sold, index funds are marketed as passively managed.

Active management solutions often charge far higher management costs than passive portfolios or funds.

Important Components of Portfolio Management

- Asset Management

The long-term mix of assets is the secret to successful portfolio management. Typically, this refers to securities such as stocks, bonds, and cash equivalents like certificates of deposit. Other options include real estate, commodities, derivatives, and cryptocurrencies. These are frequently referred to as "alternative investments."

The idea behind asset allocation is that different asset classes do not move in unison and that some are more volatile than others. A variety of investments promotes balance and reduces risk.

More aggressive investors lean more heavily toward volatile investments like growth companies in their portfolios. Investors with a cautious investment profile lean more heavily toward more reliable assets, such as bonds and reputable equities.

- Diversification

The one constant in investing is that it is impossible to anticipate winners and losers on a regular basis. The wise course of action is to assemble an investing portfolio that offers wide exposure to an asset class.

Spreading individual assets' risk and return across other asset classes or within the same asset class is known as diversification. Diversification attempts to capture the gains from all sectors over time while lowering volatility at any particular time because it is difficult to predict which subset of an asset class or sector is likely to beat another.

Real diversification involves a range of asset types, economic sectors, and geographical locations.

- Rebalancing

At regular intervals, typically once a year, rebalancing is used to bring a portfolio back to its initial target allocation. When market fluctuations knock it off balance, this is done to restore the original asset composition.

For instance, following a protracted market rally, a portfolio that initially has an allocation of 70% equities and 30% fixed income may change to an 80/20 allocation. Even if the investor has made a good profit, the portfolio now carries more risk than they are willing to take.

Selling expensive stocks and investing the proceeds in less expensive, out-of-favor equities is the overall process of rebalancing.

While maintaining the portfolio's alignment with the initial risk/return profile, the annual exercise of rebalancing enables the investor to realize gains and increase the chance for growth in high-potential sectors.

Importance of Portfolio Management

Consider a scenario in which the technology industry experiences unprecedented growth. The first month you are skeptical, the second month you start to feel more hopeful, and by the third month you are regretting not jumping on the boom. So you make the conscious decision to invest heavily in the industry in the fourth month. You make a big financial gain the next month and are overjoyed with your choice. As a result, you proceed to make more investments in the industry. By the twelfth month, you are completely immersed in one industry, but you see no problem in doing so because your profit margins are so high. But in the thirteenth month, it becomes clear that the industry's spectacular development was founded on a bubble, and within a few days, practically all of your investment is lost. This narrative is regrettable but realistic.

This is when portfolio management becomes crucial. In the first place, what precisely is a portfolio? Basically, a portfolio is a collection of financial instruments, such as stocks, mutual funds, commodities, and so forth. To put it simply, it's a detailed account of everything you've invested in the past and have right now. Consequentially, planning for the future is why keeping and managing a portfolio is important. So what exactly is portfolio management? In essence, it is the process of selecting the best investing strategy to ensure that you maximize return while also minimizing any potential risk.

- The "best investment strategy" can be chosen using Portfolio Management depending on factors including age, income, risk tolerance, and investment budget.
- As the Portfolio Management process has "risk minimization" as its focus, it helps to assess the risk that has been taken.
- Because an individual's demands and preferences are taken into consideration, such as when they need the return, how much they expect the return to be, and how long of an investment period they like, "customization" is made feasible.
- Investments can be undertaken while taking tax law changes into consideration.
- Investors are subject to interest rate risk and security price risk when they invest in fixed-

income securities like preference shares, debentures, or other similar securities. Convexity or duration might be used by the Portfolio Management to protect the portfolio.

Mastering The Art Of Stock Market Investing

CHAPTER FIVE
MAKING STOCK MARKET INVESTMENT

The stock market is a place to profit from the growth of businesses and the value of their shares, which are listed on a company's stock exchange. Many account holders learn about investing in the markets through their employer's retirement plan or through their college investment courses.

Stock market trading is a popular way of earning money in the stock market. Through investing and trading, you can earn profits by investing your money and applying your own knowledge about the financial markets.

Making stock market investments is a great way to earn money from home. Opening a brokerage account allows you to buy and sell shares quickly and easily, without the complications of performing actions online or over the phone. Each trade on the stock exchange can be bundled up with other stocks or funds, increasing your chances of earning higher returns from your investments. A good broker will make investing easy for you.

OPENING A BROKERAGE ACCOUNT

Stocks, bonds, mutual funds, and ETFs can all be purchased and sold using a brokerage account, which is an investment account. You are free to utilize your savings whenever and however you like, whether you are saving money for the future or putting money aside for a significant purchase.

Assets including stocks, bonds, mutual funds, and ETFs can be traded via a brokerage account. Many brokerage firms provide brokerage accounts, ranging from expensive full-service stockbrokers to low-cost internet bargain brokers.

- Key Lessons

There are several important measures you should take before opening a brokerage account, despite the abundance of options and the simplicity of opening an account online.

Choose the sort of broker you require, along with the features and price range they offer.

Choose the option that best represents your feelings after you've reduced your options.

Once the application process is complete, fund your account and start trading.

- Select the Type of Brokerage Account You Need

Think about your investing style when picking a broker. Would you like to stay current on the markets every day? Alternately, are you more of a "set it and forget it" investor?

Think about the asset classes you are familiar with trading or wish to learn to trade if you want to continue participating in the markets. Stocks, exchange-traded funds (ETFs), and/or mutual funds are what the majority of investors own. If you're considering trading options, you can find a number of self-directed online brokers with a variety of tools that will aid you in selecting the best approaches. The Options Basics course on Investopedia can teach you about some extremely conservative income-generating methods, even though trading options is generally thought to be riskier than trading stocks and ETFs.

Online fixed-income investments are available from many brokers, who also offer bond screeners and other portfolio-building tools.

You should give a financial advisor or a robo-advisory service serious consideration if you want to invest money but not time in accumulating wealth. Robo-advisors ask you how much money you plan to invest as well as a few questions about your time horizon and risk tolerance. If your retirement is decades away, you could be more inclined to invest in riskier asset classes than you would be if you needed to use your funds within the next three years.

Additionally, you must determine whether to form an individual retirement account or a conventional taxable account (IRA). Another choice to make concerns the ownership of the account: are you creating an account only for yourself, or will there be additional owners (such as a partner or child) who have access to it as well? You have the option of starting a custodial account or a tax-advantaged tuition account, also known as a 529 Savings Account, if you're opening an account to help a minor save for college.

- Take into account the features and associated costs that you want.

There is a lot of attention paid to the normal costs for making stock trades, but there are other benefits to using an online broker than just paying fees. The majority of online brokers eliminated equity trading costs and per-leg option commissions in the fourth quarter of 2019, which effectively put an end to much of that debate. On most options trades, you will still be required to pay commissions based on the number of contracts, and most brokers charge commissions ranging from $0.10 to $0.65 per contract.

But some "free" trades have a hidden cost. You will generally receive less-than-ideal fills for your transactions because the broker must make money somewhere and research and news coverage are scant (and occasionally nonexistent). Free trades are often covered by routing to market makers, who reimburse the broker for order volume but do not place a high priority on price improvement.

Therefore, if you are new to investing or want to improve your investment skills, opt for a broker with research and education features. The recognition of this group's members is based on their accessibility, transparent commission and pricing structures, portfolio construction tools, and research resources.

- Decide which brokerage best meets your needs

Don't be afraid to use the chat feature offered by many brokers to ask their support agents additional, in-depth questions. You can choose to call a support line for new clients, which will enable you to assess the caliber of the assistance offered.

- Start the application process

You still have to deal with the formalities of opening an account after choosing a broker.

Mastering The Art Of Stock Market Investing

You must have certain information on hand before beginning the account opening procedure, regardless of the company or type of account you select. In addition to basic information about you and other account holders like your social security number, birthdate, and address, you'll also be questioned about your job status. You must have your passport and residency visa on hand if you are a U.S. resident but not a citizen.

The "Know Your Client" regulations, which aim to stop money laundering and the support of terrorism, require brokers to gather additional data in order to comply with them. Additionally, they must confirm that you are who you claim to be in order to prevent identity theft.

Some of the questions could come off as intrusive, but U.S.-registered brokers are required to ask them in order to help the company build a profile of your expertise and experience in investing, ensuring that you invest in asset classes you are familiar with. The information the broker can show you is also governed by the regulations. Brokers must classify self-directed investors before they can receive certain sorts of advice; therefore, the questions they ask assist in this process.

You'll be questioned about your attitude toward accepting financial risks as well as how long you anticipate holding the investments. This profile includes information on your tax status, such as single or married filing jointly, and any other assets you may have, such as a home, a bank account, or an employer-sponsored retirement plan. Also required is the range of your yearly revenue. You don't need to worry about being 100% precise with your answers here. Throughout your partnership, brokers are not required to confirm or update this information. Even so, you may always return to the site's profile section and modify your answers if your circumstances change, particularly if you wish to access other asset classes.

If you don't feel comfortable sharing this kind of information online, you can download and print a paper application that you'll need to fill out and mail back. However, doing so may cause a delay of at least one week in the creation of your account. You could also open your account in person by going to a branch of one of the brokers with a physical location. However, the websites created by brokers are quite secure and offer the quickest method of opening and funding an account.

- Start Investing in Your New Account and Fund It

You can create your online login credentials, such as your user ID and password, after your account is open.

You'll need to add money to your account before you can begin trading. There are a few things you can do here, but connecting a bank account to your brokerage account is by far the simplest. Both your account number, which is often ten digits long, and the nine-digit routing number for your bank are required. The routing number can be found on a check, on the website of your bank, or by utilizing the routing number lookup tool on the American Bankers Association website.

The opening of your account will be delayed by about a week if you write a check and send it. The benefit of connecting your bank and brokerage accounts is the simplicity of money transfers. By law, U.S.-based brokers are prohibited from letting you fund a brokerage account with a credit card.

A regular monthly transfer of money from your checking account to your brokerage account can also be set up with some brokers. This is beneficial, in our opinion, particularly for individuals who are saving for a specific objective or filling a retirement account. The best use of technology is to establish a routine of frequent deposits.

Depending on how you've decided to deposit money, there will be a delay of one day to seven days before you may begin trading after your account has been opened. By watching introduction videos and setting up your home page, utilize that time to become more acquainted with the broker's website and mobile apps. Create a watchlist of stocks and experiment with the broker's stock and fund scanners.

To deliver paper statements and confirmations, the majority of brokers now charge a nominal monthly fee of $1–$2; however, you can choose to get notifications electronically to save these costs. You should also define the kinds of emails and postal mail you want to receive from your broker and their partners in your profile.

You can start making trades as soon as your deposit appears in your new account. A toast to your financial success!

PLACING BUY AND SELL ORDERS

Beginning to purchase and sell stocks is simple, especially with the development of online trading since the turn of the century. You purchase stocks from an investing firm or a brokerage firm if you're like the great majority of traders in the United States. You speak with or meet with a stockbroker who helps you make payments to other traders and accepts your market orders. To help your broker determine your investor profile, unless you are borrowing on margin, you have a cash account with them.

Buy and Sell Orders

Trade durations, fees, and price discrepancies varied between brokers and markets. Due to the high liquidity of stocks, transactions frequently take place swiftly. Your broker will either fill your order from their own inventory or route it through a computer trading network once you place it. Your order is matched with a seller, and the exchange is then carried out.

Orders come in a variety of forms. Market orders, limit orders, and stop orders are the most typical. To purchase at the current best market price, use a market order. You can select the price for limit orders, and the order may be filled over time. Stop orders enable you to set price caps on the equities you buy.

- Market Orders

When a shareholder wants to purchase or sell a security at the current market price, the shareholder can issue a market order. Since the price represents the most recent market price, such orders are executed right away. Even though the price at which the order will be executed is not guaranteed, an investor can anticipate a guarantee of order execution in this category.

Let's say that ABC stock currently trades for Rs. 500 on the market. An investor's market order to purchase this stock will be carried out right away. No assurance can be given that the stock will be purchased at the Rs. 500 "ask" price.

The ongoing market volatility that causes prices to fluctuate every second is the cause of the potential for price differences. An investor's market order may be filled after the stock's last traded price has changed. An investor can still place a trade, however, at a price that is a little bit closer to the bid or ask price. The degree of stock liquidity also affects this.

- Limit Order

A limit order enables investors to request the purchase or sale of a stock at the price they desire. A buy limit order indicates that the investor is only willing to purchase the asset at that price or below, while a sell limit order indicates that the investor only wants to sell the security at that price or above.

Mastering The Art Of Stock Market Investing

There is no assurance that a limit order will be executed after it is placed, unlike market orders.

Let's say an investor placed a purchase limit order at Rs. 200 for a stock. This indicates that the investor will only purchase the shares at a price of Rs. 200 or less. When someone issues a sell limit order for a stock at Rs. 200, they are indicating that they will only sell the shares for Rs. 200 or more.

Investors can ensure that they don't follow stock price trends and can strive for the proper price by using this form of order. A limit order can, in some cases, aid in the automation of trades. Once placed, these kinds of orders may be valid for a trading day, a few weeks, or even a month.

- Stop Order

This kind of stock purchase or sale order is only carried out when the stock price reaches the specified price. The term "stop price" refers to such a stock price or value. This kind of order is inert until the stock price reaches the stated price. The stop order does not become a market order or limit order until the stock price is reached, at which point it is executed.

A stop-loss order is another name for this kind of order. It is particularly helpful for traders or investors who don't have the time to continuously monitor the market and make deals properly throughout the trading day.

Let's say an investor learns that a stock's price falling below Rs. 60 will probably result in a significant loss for them. He or she can use a stop order to sell the stock as soon as its price hits this level because they cannot continuously monitor the stock price. The investor can thereby avoid suffering a large loss.

MONITORING AND MANAGING INVESTMENTS

You should routinely assess your portfolio (at least once a year) to make sure it is still in accordance with your goals because the stock market is continuously changing.

Wealth planning's lifeblood is active investment monitoring, and foresight is its foundation. A portfolio's holdings may alter significantly as a result of minor market fluctuations because investing is a dynamic field. When personal ripples occur, the investor may need to realign their present and/or future interests due to changes in their circumstances.

In either case, keeping tabs on your portfolio's health is crucial. Monitoring investments well can increase wealth or prevent losses, and this involves more than just understanding the numbers. A specific mindset is necessary for successful investing in order to avoid being overconfident or concerned about cyclical shifts.

Regular market monitoring cultivates an essential trait in an investor: serenity. Markets can be tumultuous and unexpected. Individuals who monitor their investments can see how markets change over time. Exposure to this fluctuation helps investors develop a more level-headed and robust point of view because they understand that a loss need not be the end of the world and that a quick gain is not necessarily a cue to become overconfident.

Monitoring numerous assets (especially if they cross asset classes) makes people an active part of their wealth strategy and instills a greater awareness of how different classes interact and why perceptions of a weak or good return vary between markets.

Investors will inevitably compare their portfolio returns to those of others and conclude that their situation is either better or worse. Investment monitoring replaces that perspective with one that is oriented toward benchmarking. Small-cap stocks' profits and losses, for instance, don't compare well to those of large-cap companies. Bond and stock mutual funds shouldn't be compared to those that deal just in stocks or other securities.

While keeping an eye on your existing investments, cross-category comparisons might occasionally be useful. If another asset class piques your attention, you might want to monitor its performance for a period, or you might want to look at the portfolios of people who share your investment objectives. In this case, it's important to examine both the overall cyclical losses and gains and the swings' volatility.

Long- or short-term investors might use data monitoring to frequently evaluate their portfolios and interests to see how they fit with their time-based strategy.

The receipt of regular investment reports, such as those delivered monthly or quarterly, can help long-term investors relax. If you're a short-term investor, it makes sense to monitor your portfolio much more frequently. In fact, it's a necessity if your assets are on the riskier side. It could be required to provide daily or weekly updates to keep things moving in the right direction.

To realign with new aims or to stabilize the portfolio after a loss, some rebalancing may be required. By selling or purchasing asset classes to return your strategy's equilibrium, rebalancing is a powerful method of risk management for your portfolio and for keeping wise relative percentages of your investments.

Every type of investor benefits from seeing personally how fluid the markets are and making more educated choices rather than changing their strategy due to concerns for the near term. Additionally, this prevents unused taxes and transaction fees from being paid. Since troughs are frequently transient and are not a reliable indicator of performance over the long term, it may always be preferable to monitor over the long term rather than aim for short-term gains.

Additionally, monitoring clarifies expenses and offers protection against data inconsistencies. Regular updates from your wealth advisor will include analyses of all activities throughout the quarter, outlooks for the near or distant future, and thorough and transparent explanations of all fees and costs. Projections show an investment's potential in a larger market context, which can be either favorable or negative regardless of how it is performing right now. And working with an experienced advisor is necessary to receive this kind of insightful criticism.

Things to keep in mind when keeping an eye on your investments:

- Examine the returns and ask if everything is still on course to achieve your objectives as you evaluate the performance of your portfolio.
- Examine each of your particular funds; different fund managers excel under certain conditions. Your position and your investments' positions are likely to fluctuate over time. It's critical to ensure that each is operating as efficiently as possible.
- In order to keep your investing strategy balanced and in line with your risk tolerance, evaluate your asset allocation. You will also want to make sure your portfolio is appropriately diversified while doing this.
- For instance, do you have investments in other asset types or just equity funds? Will this ratio remain the same after a year if your portfolio is divided evenly between stock and bond funds? Your portfolio may change from how it started over time due to the variable performance of several funds.
- Review your long-term objectives; it's crucial to always know what they are and whether your portfolio is on track to help you reach them. For instance, if you're putting money aside for a new home, you should make sure

your portfolio is constructed for growth rather than income.

Mastering The Art Of Stock Market Investing

CHAPTER SIX
STOCK MARKET RISKS AND CHALLENGES

Market risk is the chance that a person, business, or other entity will lose money as a result of events that have an impact on how well investments perform overall in the financial markets.

- Key Lessons

Market risk, also known as systematic risk, has an immediate impact on all market activity.

Diversification cannot completely remove market risk.

Diversification helps reduce specific risk, also known as unsystematic risk, which is a risk related to the performance of a certain security.

Changes in interest rates, exchange rates, geopolitical crises, or recessions can all increase market risk.

MARKET VOLATILITY

The stock market is always changing. Daily gains and losses are shown in market indices; during more stable times, the S&P 500 only fluctuates by less than 1% per day. However, the market occasionally encounters abrupt price shifts, or "volatility," which is a phenomenon.

In long-term investing, increased volatility is all but inevitable and may even be one of the keys to success. While it might be a sign of difficulty, it can also be a sign of success.

The frequency and size of price changes, whether they are up or down, are considered market volatility. The greater the size and frequency of price movements, the more volatile the market is said to be.

According to Nicole Gopoian Wirick, CFP, creator of Prosperity Wealth Strategies in Birmingham, Michigan, "market volatility is a normal element of investment and is to be expected in a portfolio." If markets moved straight up, then investing would be simple and we'd all be wealthy.

Dealing with Market Volatility

You have a plethora of options for responding to the ups and downs of your portfolio. One thing is for sure, though: After a significant market decline, experts do not advise panic selling.

According to experts at the Schwab Center for Financial Research, in the periods since 1970 when equities had falls of 20% or more, they produced the most gains in the first year of recovery. Thus, your assets would have missed out on big recoveries and may never have done so if you had left at the bottom and then waited to return.

Instead, consider one of these strategies when the market volatility has you on edge:

- Keep in Mind Your Long-Term Plan

A well-diversified, well-balanced portfolio was really created with times like these in mind because investing is a long-term endeavor. If you're going to need money soon, you shouldn't put it on the market, where volatility makes it difficult to get rid of it quickly. But for long-term objectives, volatility is a necessary step on the road to considerable development.

The cost of investing in assets that provide you with the highest chance of achieving long-term goals is volatility, according to Gage Paul, CFP, a financial counselor in Hudson, Ohio. It is to be anticipated and can be seen as a cost in achieving these objectives.

- Seek Opportunities in Market Volatility

Thinking about how much stock you can buy while the market is in a bearish downward situation may assist you cope psychologically with market volatility.

Mastering The Art Of Stock Market Investing

Periods of volatility actually give us a chance to buy these equities at a reduced price, adds Garcia, especially in the case of stocks that have been strong over the preceding few years.

For example, after more than a decade of steady growth, you could have purchased shares of an S&P 500 index fund for about a third of the price they were a month earlier during the bear market of 2020. Your investment would have increased by 14% from the start of the year and around 65% from its low by the end of the year.

- Ensure a Stable Emergency Fund

Since you might have to sell assets in a bear market, market volatility isn't a problem unless you need to liquidate an investment. Investors should pay special attention to building an emergency reserve that is equivalent to three to six months' worth of living expenses.

For clients to not have to worry about selling investments to cover cash demands during times of market turbulence, Wirick says they set aside a suitable emergency fund. Clients' minds are at ease because of this.

Planners advise having up to two years' worth of non-market-connected assets if you're approaching retirement. Bonds, cash, cash value in life insurance, home equity lines of credit, and home equity conversion mortgages all fall under this category.

When the market is down, Benjamin Offit, CFP, a financial advisor in Towson, Maryland, advises investors to take money out of stocks and wait for the market to recover before selling their portfolio.

- Your portfolio should be rebalanced as necessary.

As a result of market volatility, which can result in abrupt changes in investment values, it's possible that, following periods of rapid movements in either direction, your asset allocation will veer away from your targeted divides.

To get your portfolio back in line with your investing objectives and the level of risk you prefer at these periods, rebalance it. When you rebalance, sell some of the asset class that has migrated to a larger part of your portfolio than you'd like and use the proceeds to acquire more of the asset class that has been too small. When your allocation deviates from your original goal mix by at least 5%, it's a good idea to rebalance.

If you notice a variation of more than 20% in an asset class, you might also want to rebalance. For instance, if you wanted emerging market equities to make up 10% of your portfolio but, following a significant market fluctuation, found that they made up more like 8% or 12%, you may want to adjust your holdings.

ECONOMIC AND POLITICAL FACTORS AFFECTING THE STOCK MARKET.

There are a few signs to help you get a sense of what might be ahead, even if it's impossible to completely foresee the stock market or time the ideal plan. Stock prices are influenced by some economic aspects, giving you a hint as to what might come next. Because firm profitability depends on the health of the economy, economic news is important to the stock market. Many organizations with stock market shares rely on a favorable economic environment. More individuals are spending money and are more likely to invest while the economy is growing. The stock prices are supported by everything mentioned. As a result, businesses and their stocks experience a fall in value when the economy is struggling. Observe the following five factors:

Economic Factors

- Amounts of interest

Rates of interest are one element that affects stock prices. A higher cost of borrowing money reduces firm profit margins when interest rates are higher. Stock prices are likely to decline as profits decline. A reduction in interest rates, which makes borrowing money less expensive, frequently boosts the economy when stock values are falling and the economy is hurting. Though not always the case, this is the case in this instance. The recent Federal Reserve interest rate drop was deemed insufficient, which had little positive impact on the stock market.

- Inflation (and deflation).

The stock market is affected by price pressure as well. Things become more expensive as a result of inflation or upward price pressure. High inflation reduces purchasing power to the point that fears that businesses may hoard cash arise. On the other hand, deflation is regarded as being just as serious a concern. Although decreasing prices provide consumers with more purchasing power, deflation is actually viewed as a major indicator of an impending economic catastrophe. It is seen as beneficial to have some inflation, but not too much. Utilizing interest rates as a tool to maintain inflation in a "manageable" range is one of the Federal Reserve's primary responsibilities.

- GDP

GDP, commonly referred to as gross domestic product, is a peculiar creature when it comes to the stock market. Stock prices often benefit when the GDP reading is higher because increased economic activity inspires optimism. The consequent rise in spending and sales brought on by the optimism has continued to raise the GDP. On the other hand, a GDP result that is lower than anticipated may be a sign of things to come. When confidence declines, stock prices can follow suit. The cycle may repeat again if the stock market falls, prompting actions that have an influence on GDP.

- Unemployment

It's crucial to understand that unemployment is a lagging sign for stocks when considering it. As a result, it's frequently taken as a sign that something is already wrong with the economy. By the time the unemployment rate declines, economic conditions will probably have changed. The stock market may suffer, though, if the unemployment rate is higher than anticipated when it is released. People who are looking for work but are unable to find it are indicated by a high unemployment rate. When unemployment rises, so does confidence in the economy, and stock values often fall as well.

- War on trade

After fresh tariffs on China went into effect on August 1 and the trade battle heated up, the Dow Jones Industrial Average dropped more than 300 points and then more than 750 points. Trade conflicts and tariffs are problematic in part because they increase costs for American businesses. When they import goods from other nations, they must pay greater taxes. They must choose whether to pass the expense onto customers based on how long the tariffs are in effect. Slower economic growth can result from high consumer expenses that inhibit purchasing. However, corporations experience a decline in their profit margins when they don't pass the costs on to customers. Trade wars have an effect on the economy and can influence stock prices, even if their effects may not be long-lasting.

Political factors

- Geopolitical

The previous few years have seen an increased focus on international government relations, with international cooperation on COVID-19 bringing some states together and dividing others.

The de facto lines of allegiance may have been drawn through COVID-19, but energy and supply chain security have attempted to erase them.

The reality that awaits the countries emerging from COVID-19 hibernation is substantially different; long-term trading partners and foreign direct investment partners have been fundamentally replaced.

The petrodollar agreement from the Nixon period is nearing its end as the US moves toward becoming a large oil exporter in direct conflict with the recently created OPEC+ group.

By utilizing Chevron Corp. (NYSE: CVX) to increase oil production in OPEC member Venezuela, just as OPEC seeks to reduce output within its own organization, the United States is redefining its relationship with OPEC+. Saudi Arabia has reacted by turning to the east to negotiate a deal with China akin to the multi-decade agreement that existed during the Nixon administration.

This change in global politics will have long-lasting effects on the Middle East and beyond.

With the east becoming increasingly dependent on the European and LATAM markets, this will be felt most acutely by the US producers and refiners, who are no longer functioning in a favorable relationship.

In the following months and years, the European market's primary strategy will be to drastically reduce its dependency on oil. The greatest years for Gulf of Mexico refiners Valero Corp (NYSE:VLO; VLO) and Phillips 66 (NYSE:PSX; PSX) may be behind them as a result of this change.

Doors opening to investment opportunities will often close under the pretext of political fortunes because geopolitical demarcation lines are quite changeable. Because of this, fundamental company research and the effects of politics within limits continue to be the strongest sources for making investment judgments.

One can anticipate that geopolitical fortunes will have a significant impact on the stock market in the years to come because the future of the global order appears to be less assured than it has been in the previous 70 years.

- Fiscal policy

The current tax policy has by far the most overall direct impact on corporate profits and, consequently, firm valuations.

The corporate tax rate in the UK has increased from 19% to 25%. Such a sharp increase underscores the UK government's need to implement austerity measures as it fights rising prices and the negative consequences of Brexit.

Business leaders appreciated the clarity, and the announcement assisted in stabilizing the pound and the larger economy by outlining a clear course of action for the Rishi Sunak administration.

The frequently criticized "carried-interest loophole" still exists in the US. Over the past ten years, private equity has expanded into the energy, technology, and real estate sectors.

On the plus side, the boom in private equity has made it possible to fully utilize intellectual property, creating thousands of jobs in the process. Those jobs will probably be at risk from any bipartisan effort to fix the loophole because of worries about a budget imbalance.

Corporate investment and expansion may be less favorable under reduced return criteria brought about by greater taxes as worldwide government budgets become stressed from high prices and move toward an austerity stance.

The corporate environment in the UK, Europe, and the US, as well as general employment, are expected to be affected by higher corporation taxes paired with the exclusion of private equity from the lower taxes offered by the carried-interest loophole.

- Regulation

Financial regulation has many different forms, and it includes laws that are designed to safeguard a variety of stakeholders, including consumers, investors, state electorates, and others.

Unless one has a thorough comprehension of the regulation and its alleged influence, the depth and breadth of regulations are huge and challenging to transfer into any useful study.

That being said, some sectors of business and finance are ready for new rules, either due to the bad behavior of the people involved or to the industry's now disproportionately large impact on important stakeholders, which justifies the construction of safeguards.

There will undoubtedly be new laws adopted around the world as a result of the FTX crash. New regulation aimed at safeguarding cryptocurrency investors will probably be introduced as a result of the extent and scope of the losses brought on by what appears to be huge corporate misconduct.

If you have a current investment in participants in the crypto market who are most likely to be influenced by new rules, it is important to keep in mind that legislation frequently has an unintended effect. This group will undoubtedly include centralized exchanges such as Coinbase Global, Inc. (NASDAQ:COIN) (COIN).

Technology and data privacy are certain to experience a change in rules in 2023. To the dismay of Meta Platforms, Inc. (NASDAQ:META), Europe has already experienced a substantial movement toward the GDPR, a law that prioritizes consumer privacy. The types of data and market size that social data-harvesting businesses like META and Snap Inc NYSE:SNAP collect could be significantly impacted by the policy's expansion to US soil (SNAP).

Consideration has already been given to new comprehensive consumer privacy laws in Connecticut, California, Virginia, Colorado, Utah, and Colorado. If the improvements are well-liked, advocates may gain support through a federal mandate, but nothing is currently planned.

A federal data privacy law may be able to restrict the data collection methods used by a number of well-known social media sites. If state legislation is implemented, it will undoubtedly affect corporation valuations, which is something to watch out for.

- Action Switch

Recent European and American leadership and mid-term elections generated a lot of discussion about a predicted tilt to the right of the political spectrum. While the so-called "red wave" was more of a trickle in the US, the conservative parties prevailed in Italy and Sweden.

Democratic control of the Senate coexists with a narrow Republican victory in the US House of Representatives. A centered liberal democracy is still very much required in Europe and the US.

Suppose that escalating geopolitical threats are receiving more attention. In those circumstances, it appears likely that the more nationalistic element will keep winning over votes under the flag of strength and security.

Generally speaking, conservative and right-leaning voters favor greater self-reliance

lesser government spending, more powerful armed forces, and fewer taxes.

As defense companies like Lockheed Martin and BAE Systems PLC (LSE:BAE) find their wallets stuffed with government spending, these themes may be reflected in the stock market.

If higher interest rates are used outside of defense, it will make governments' balance sheets smaller and may even help the financial sector, assuming that credit quality doesn't degrade too much. Such an economic environment will be favored by banks like Lloyds Banking Group plc (LSE:LLOY) and JP Morgan Chase & Co (NYSE:JPM).

PROTECTING AGAINST LOSS IN THE STOCK MARKET

Particularly if one maintains a moderately risky profile, a stock market crash, a steep market correction, or a quick collapse caused by an unanticipated bad event in the economy and the stock market in general can result in drastic losses in the portfolio.

"The more volatile and significant losses that a portfolio is susceptible to in unfavorable circumstances, the riskier it is".

Nevertheless, volatility poses a risk to all assets, including real estate, commodities, currencies, cryptocurrencies, and even "conservative" bonds. It is important to note that volatility is not just a problem for traditional stock markets.

- Stock exchange

The simplest method to reduce losses and changes in overall wealth is unquestionably by selling or downsizing possessions and turning them into cash.

Mastering The Art Of Stock Market Investing

Additionally, it can be the best investment plan for your risk profile.

Selling is obviously preferable to holding declining stocks in severe circumstances with significant downward market moves and/or with limited understanding of how to hedge one's portfolio.

- Using diversification to hedging

You can also pick the route of diversification and sell a portion of your stock holdings and reinvest the proceeds in bonds, real estate, or other assets if you are no longer certain whether an asset class, like stocks, will soon experience a correction.

It can drastically cut losses.

The new asset classes' negative correlation is what you need to focus on the most, though.

As a result, the diversification assets should not react similarly to the securities whose risk in the total portfolio is to be decreased in the case of a crash.

Simply put, it only makes sense to add an "A" to a "B" if "A" crashes and "B" at best remains neutral.

Diversification is useless if the correlation between the two assets is 1:1 and they both fall at the same rate.

- Using certificates for reverse bonus hedging

Although they seem difficult, reverse bonus certificates are extremely simple to explain.

A great approach to protect stock investments from losses is with reverse bonus certificates.

These certificates can virtually entirely hedge the stock position, depending on the amount invested.

These certificates have the benefit of being able to generate gains even in the event that market trends are slightly upward or sideways and an impending crash or market correction is therefore misjudged.

- Direct hedging using puts and mini-futures shorts on short certificates

Nearly every popular single value, not just indices, has a suitable short instrument, or security, that allows one to speculate on the underlying dropping prices.

If you wish to hedge specific assets in your portfolio or only certain components of an asset class, such as precious metals for commodities, it can be quite helpful.

This type of hedging performs superbly when used with stock shares as well.

When the oil price drops at the same time and you believe there is a high likelihood of low oil prices, you can only specifically hedge that sector. For instance, if the technological sector continues to perform well, you don't hedge these. with shorts on the big oil index, the oil price, the oil price ETF, or all three in this instance.

There are two methods for selling these securities short:

Sell 200 shares of the oil ETF short, for example, in order to sell short the securities in the quantity necessary to cover your other position; or

Purchase enough puts (1 contract is equal to 100 shares) to cover your position (for example, buy 2 puts on the oil index with expiration in 3 months).

The benefit of buying a put over a short position is that the former has a restricted negative risk and the latter an endless one.

If the stock price or index falls below a certain level established by the particular put option parameters, the value of the corresponding put option contract rises.

Puts are used to protect against falls in specific stocks or to cover the entire stock market through options on ETFs.

Put options allow investors to make some profits if, instead of going down, the portfolio rises by more than what has been paid for the puts because only the money paid for option contracts is at risk.

- Hedging the portfolio's risk in part permanently

It is also feasible to permanently hedge your assets, but is it even conceivable?

Since you would not have purchased these shares for the long term if you did not anticipate greater share prices and, thus, profits at the end, it would seem counterintuitive to permanently hedge them in every stock market phase if you buy shares for the long run.

A low-cost short ETF on the S&P 500 index, for example, can be an effective way to permanently hedge throughout the course of the holding period.

Investors who do not want to experience significant stock price volatility may find this particularly intriguing.

The hedges will lessen both the performance at the conclusion of the anticipated holding period and the variations over the whole holding period.

As an illustration, you might purchase an S&P500 ETF and initially hedge it short with an S&P500 ETF by depleting 50% of its value. The portfolio will only see a 25% loss if the S&P500 loses 50% of its value.

It's possible that you would have kept the remaining 50% in the account as cash and just invested 50% in the ETF previously.

The short ETF, however, gains a lot in this instance and can be invested back into the S&P500. The permanent hedge is once more personal as well.

Though it obviously does not ensure it, a 50% plunge in the S&P500 lowers the static likelihood of another 50% collapse. Now that the S&P500 may be permanently hedged with only 20% of the risk through a short ETF, you can benefit more from an increase without taking on more risk.

- Reduce the stocks' cost base.

On a cost basis, how much of your money is involved in the position?

Your cost basis is $33, for instance, if you paid $33 for 100 shares of stock. The cost basis would then drop to $32 if a dividend payment of $1 was made over the course of your investment. You are only putting $32 a share at risk at this point if the stock declines.

In the previous example with dividends, the cost basis decreased extremely slowly. If the market is moving downward, the stock price may fall more quickly than the dividend can lower your cost basis.

What if your cost basis could be reduced even more quickly?

Writing covered calls is a solution.

You receive the option premium as cash in your account when you write a covered call on your stock position (one contract for every 100 shares you own). Your cost basis is further reduced in this manner.

This lowers your risk on the downside but caps your potential upside.

You won't be able to take advantage of every one of these possible advantages if the stock appreciates dramatically. But hey, a smaller potential profit comes at the cost of lower risk.

Over time, it is feasible to reduce the cost basis for long-term holdings to zero. This indicates that the position no longer costs you anything because you have returned all of its capital. This indicates that there is no downside risk.

CHAPTER SEVEN
ADVANCED STOCK MARKET STRATEGIS

SHORT SELLING

The goal of the short-selling technique is to make money when the value of an asset declines. Short sellers start by selling an item and then buying it back later, preferably at a lower price, in contrast to most investors, who purchase an asset and then sell it for a profit.

A sophisticated trading technique known as "short selling" turns the notion of investment on its head. Going long in the stock market refers to buying a stock with the intention of selling it for a profit at a later date. When a trader "goes short," they are betting that the price of the stock will fall.

To start a short position on a stock, a trader borrows shares from a broker and then immediately sells that position in the market to other buyers.

The short seller must repurchase the shares to conclude the trade and pay back the broker for the lent funds, ideally at a lower price. If, as anticipated, the stock's price declined, the trader would benefit from the price difference after deducting costs and interest.

Trading on decreasing prices or hedging a position are two things that can be done by using the approach known as "selling short." Short selling may seem simple, but there are several hazards involved.

Even without accounting for the costs associated with borrowing shares, the short seller will lose money if the price of the stock increases rather than declines.

To be eligible to engage in short selling, you must open a margin account with a broker. The first phase of the strategy—borrowing a stock—entails additional costs.

How do short sales operate?

How does shorting a stock work? A trading tactic to make money when a stock's price drops is short selling. While it can appear straightforward in theory, traders should use caution.

When asset values are decreasing, it can be challenging to recognize profitable trading opportunities. As a result, short selling is often a short-term strategy that is favored mostly by day traders.

Trading short needs traders to adopt a different perspective from traditional "buy and hold" investors on specific assets or the market.

Short sellers must be at ease adopting a naturally gloomy stance in opposition to the market's predominating upward inclination. Because short sellers concentrate on tactics that are unpopular with the majority of market participants, short selling frequently correlates with contrarian investment.

Traders frequently concentrate on fundamental analysis of a company's financials to find potential future sources of weakness for the stock, technical analysis of the stock's historical trading patterns, or developing a case for thematic weakness that will affect a sector of stocks when looking into potential candidates for a short sale. Some traders will short a stock, while others will use exchange-traded fund trading tactics to short the market as a whole (ETFs).

In the event that prices decline, some traders will utilize short selling as a hedge to reduce losses on an existing long position. While shorting a stock involves the same basic principles, the end result is considerably different. Depending on whether prices rise or fall, using short selling as part of a hedging plan might help protect some gains or reduce losses.

How to Sell a Stock Short

While purchasing a stock only requires a few quick clicks, there are additional processes needed to short a stock. Most investors also aren't able to decide to start shorting stocks out of the blue. Here is a step-by-step tutorial on shorting stocks:

- Get a margin account set up with your broker. A margin account is necessary for short selling since it enables you to borrow money to purchase stocks. The Financial Industry Regulatory Authority, generally known as FINRA, has established minimum conditions that must be met before you may begin trading on margin. Notably, federal law often mandates that short sellers maintain a margin account balance with a starting balance equivalent to 150% of the value of the equities they are short, with a maintenance requirement that is typically 30%.
- Find candidates for short sales. Once your broker has given you the go-ahead to short a stock, you must find an opportunity by researching equities. A strong thesis for why the stock's price would decline must be developed, one that is supported by a comprehensive examination of the firm and its stock, due to the possibility of losses.
- Create a strategy for the short-selling trade. Prior to carrying out any component of the transaction, you should make a plan to enter

the trade and, more crucially, to exit the deal at a profit, accounting for commissions and interest paid on the amount borrowed. Since a short sale is based on the premise that prices will decline, you should also have a backup strategy in place in case the stock's price increases to limit losses.

- Implement the short sale. Once the aforementioned tasks have been completed, it's time to fund your wager. It could be simpler to execute a deal as intended without letting emotions influence your choices if you use stop orders for trading.

Short-Selling Risks

The most obvious danger connected with short selling is that the price of an asset rises when a trader expects it to fall.

The longer you wait for a trade to turn profitable, the more interest you have to pay on your margin account, and the more risk you take on in the event that the price keeps increasing. You might also need to add extra money to your margin account in order to prevent a "margin call," which happens when the value of the securities in your account drops below a set threshold.

The last risk related to short selling is short squeezes. This occurs when the price of a stock that has been widely shorted rises, putting pressure on short sellers to exit their positions in order to prevent losses. By doing this, short sellers who have already purchased the shares can stimulate more stock price gains.

Due to the dangers of short selling and the requirement for margin, many traders would like to stay away from adopting this complex trading technique.

A less risky option on the options market is to buy put options, which provide the trader with the right but not the obligation to sell the underlying stock at a specific price in the future. This options strategy offers traders a way to speculate on falling prices with less risk.

OPTION TRADING

Investors can speculatively predict the future course of the entire stock market or specific instruments, such as stocks or bonds, through the use of options trading. The opportunity to buy or sell an underlying asset at a specific price by a specified date is provided by options contracts, but it's not a legal requirement.

What Kinds of Choices Are There?

Without having to actually purchase the speculative asset in question, investors can use options as tradable contracts to make predictions about whether its price will be greater or lower at a specific point in the future.

For instance, Nifty 50 options give investors the chance to opine on the potential course of this benchmark stock index, which is sometimes seen as a proxy for the Indian stock market as a whole.

Options initially look a little counterintuitive, but they aren't as difficult as they seem.

Several key phrases are all you need to comprehend options:

Derivative. Options are a type of derivative, which means that the value of an option is derived from another asset. Consider stock options, where the price of a particular stock determines the option contract's value.

Strike price and the date of expiration. A striking price is the predetermined price that was discussed earlier. Until the expiration date of an option contract, traders may exercise the option at the strike price.

Premium. A premium is the cost associated with buying an option, and it is determined by taking into account the value and price of the underlying security.

Both intrinsic and extrinsic values exist. The difference between the strike price and current value of the underlying asset in an option contract is known as intrinsic value. Extrinsic value refers to other elements that influence the premium but are not included in

intrinsic value, such as the expiration date of the option.

Both profitable and unsuccessful. An option is considered to be in-the-money (profitable) or out-of-the-money (unprofitable) depending on the price of the underlying securities and the time until expiration (unprofitable).

Types Of Options

Various Options: Calls and Puts

Derivative securities include options. Because its price is inextricably tied to the price of another thing, an option is a derivative. The right, but not the duty, to buy or sell an underlying asset at a predetermined price on or before a specific date is provided by purchasing an options contract.

The right to acquire a stock is provided by a call option, while the right to sell a stock is provided by a put option. A call option might be compared to a deposit for a future acquisition.

"Options are not right for everyone since they include risks. Trading options has a considerable risk of loss and can be considered speculative."

- Call Option

A call option provides the right but not the duty to purchase the underlying security at the strike price on or before expiration. Therefore, if the price of the underlying security rises, the value of a call option will increase (calls have a positive delta).

Since a long call has an unlimited upside potential but a maximum loss equal to the premium (price) paid for the option, it can be used to speculate on the price of the underlying going up.

Consider a call option.

A prospective homeowner notices a new construction project being built. In the future, that person might want the option to buy a house, but they won't want to use it until certain nearby developments are complete.

The decision of whether to buy or not would be advantageous to the potential homeowner. Consider the possibility that they may purchase a call option from the developer to purchase the house for, let's say, $400,000 at any time over the course of the following three years. They certainly can—known it's as a non-refundable deposit. Naturally, the developer wouldn't provide such a choice without charging. To secure that right, the prospective homeowner must put down money.

This expense is referred to as the "premium" in relation to an option. It is the option contract's cost. The deposit in our hypothetical home example could be $20,000, which the buyer gives to the developer. Consider a scenario in which the developments are complete and the zoning has been approved after two years. Because that is the amount specified in the contract, the homebuyer exercises the option and purchases the property for $400,000.

- Put Option

A put option, as contrasted to a call option, gives the holder the choice—but not the obligation—to sell the underlying stock at the strike price on or before the expiration date. Because the option increases in value when the underlying's price decreases, a long put is consequently a short position in the underlying securities (they have a negative delta). Protective puts can be bought as a kind of insurance, giving investors a price floor to hedge their positions.

Consider a Put Option

A put option can now be compared to an insurance policy. You are probably already familiar with the procedure for buying homeowner's insurance if you own your home. To guard against damage to their home, a homeowner purchases a homeowner's policy. They pay a sum known as a premium for a specific period of time, say a year. The insurance holder is protected by the policy in the event that the residence is destroyed and has a face value.

What if your asset was an investment in stocks or an index rather than a house? In a similar vein, an investor can buy put options to insure their holdings in the S&P 500 index. Investors who believe a bear market is imminent may be reluctant to liquidate more than 10% of their long positions in the S&P 500 index due to this worry. They can buy a put option entitling them to sell the S&P 500 index, for instance, at $2,250 at any time over the following two years if it is now trading at $2,500.

By being able to sell the index for $2,250 while it is trading at $2,000—a cumulative loss of just 10%—they will have made 250 points if the market drops by 20% in six months (500 points on the index). In fact, if this put option is kept, even if the market collapses to zero, the loss would only be 10%. Again, buying the option will incur a cost (the premium), and if the market doesn't decline over that time, the option's maximum loss will be limited to the premium paid.

Applications of Call and Put Options

Different conditions call for the usage of call options and put options. Some use cases for call and put options are shown below.

Call option buyers use them as a hedge against their position in the event that the price of the security or commodity falls.

Put option buyers use them as a hedge against their position in the event that the price of the security or commodity rises.

To protect themselves from a drop in their purchasing power, American importers can use call options on the US currency.

American exporters can use put options on the dollar to protect themselves from an increase in their selling prices.

ADR (American Depository Receipt) holders in overseas corporations can use call options on the dollar to protect themselves from a drop in dividend payments.

To protect themselves from a drop in the value of their home currency for payment, international manufacturers can employ put options on the US dollar.

Call options are used by short sellers as a hedge against their bets.

Given that a stock's price can never go below zero, short sellers can only profit on put options to a certain extent.

DIVERSIFICATION AND ASSET ALLOCATION

Avoid putting all of your eggs in one basket. That axiom neatly distills the ideas behind asset allocation and diversification.

Determining how many of your eggs you're going to place into how many various baskets, or asset classes, is the investment counterpart of asset allocation. Spreading out your investments across several asset classes is what is meant by diversification. Additionally, rebalancing entails making periodic adjustments to make sure that you continue to meet your goal allocation over time. All are crucial instruments for controlling investment risk.

Variety is the key to these tactics. Asset allocation, diversification, and rebalancing should, if done correctly, produce a balanced mix of lifetime performance and risk protection.

Making an asset allocation decision is the first step. Your asset allocation is the percentage of your overall portfolio that you will invest in various asset classes, such as equities, bonds, cash, and cash equivalents. These investments can be made directly by acquiring certain securities or indirectly by selecting funds that hold those equities. Options, futures, commodities, real estate, and more are among the asset groups that some investors also take into account.

Investments fall into various kinds, each of which has a different response to shifting political and economic conditions. By adding a variety of asset classes to your portfolio, you raise the likelihood that some of your investments may generate respectable returns even when others are flat or declining in value.

Your investing horizon and risk tolerance are only two of the variables that will affect how you allocate your assets. Additionally, you can have various accounts with various goal asset allocations. For instance, if you're about to buy a house, you might invest more heavily in cash or cash equivalents in your down payment fund, but if retirement is still decades away, you might invest more heavily in stocks in your retirement fund.

To manage risk effectively, asset allocation is insufficient on its own. After all, investing all of your money entirely in a single class of securities won't provide much protection. Instead, it puts your attention in danger. Diversification has a role in this.

Regardless of how resilient you may expect a particular security or asset class to be, diversification lowers the danger of significant losses that can arise from overemphasizing it. This is particularly true if the assets in your portfolio are "uncorrelated," which means they respond to economic events differently from one another. Holding both of these asset types (as well as others) might help with risk management because, for example, stocks and bonds frequently move in opposite directions from one another. Playing the Field: Diversification is a Smart Investing Course where you may learn more.

Diversification among and within asset classes is typically advised by financial professionals. When you hold many stocks, for instance, your level of diversification increases when it comes to stocks. It rises even more when those stocks are diversified geographically, contain a variety of industries (including technology, consumer, healthcare, and more), and are made up of small, medium, and large companies (domestic and international).

Similar to this, if you were to buy bonds, you might select them from various issuers, including the federal government, state and local governments, and corporations, as well as those with various terms and credit ratings.

Many investors use pooled investments, such as mutual funds and exchange-traded funds, to create a diversified portfolio. In order to spread your risk, pooled investments often involve more and a wider range of underlying investments than you're likely to put together on your own. However, you must ensure that your investments—including those in pools—are diversified. Owning two mutual funds that invest in the same subclass of equities, for instance, won't aid in your diversification.

CHAPTER EIGHT
CONCLUSION

In conclusion, "Navigating The Stock Market: Tips for Successful Investing" has provided a comprehensive overview of the fundamental concepts and tools that investors can use to get started in the stock market. We've covered the key drivers of stock prices, including economic indicators, company earnings, and market news. We've also introduced the concept of technical analysis and how it can be used to interpret market trends. By the end of this guide, you should have a solid understanding of the basics of investing and be well-equipped to begin your journey in the stock market. Remember, investing carries inherent risks and there are no guarantees of success. However, by staying informed, diversifying your portfolio, and maintaining a long-term perspective, you can increase your chances of success as an investor.

As you continue to learn and grow as an investor, it's important to stay up-to-date on market developments and to be open to new ideas and strategies. Investing is a constantly evolving field, and what works in one market environment may not be as effective in another. By staying open to new ideas and approaches, you can better position yourself for success in the stock market.

Mastering The Art Of Stock Market Investing

In addition to staying informed, it's also important to diversify your portfolio and consider the potential risks and rewards of each investment. By including a mix of assets in your portfolio, you can help to mitigate the impact of any single market event and increase your chances of long-term success.

Finally, it's essential to have a well-defined investment strategy and to stick to it. This can help you stay focused and avoid impulsive or emotional decision-making. By maintaining a long-term perspective and staying disciplined, you can better navigate the ups and downs of the market and increase your chances of success as an investor.

Overall, the key to success in the stock market is to stay informed, diversify your portfolio, and maintain a long-term perspective. By following these principles, you can increase your chances of success as an investor and work towards achieving your financial goals.

As you continue to develop your skills as an investor, it's important to regularly review and assess your portfolio to ensure it aligns with your financial goals and risk tolerance. This may involve rebalancing your portfolio to maintain your desired asset allocation, or making adjustments to your investments in light of changing market conditions or personal circumstances.

It's also important to periodically review your investment strategy and consider whether it's still aligned with your financial goals. This may involve setting new goals, adjusting your risk tolerance, or revisiting your asset allocation. By regularly reviewing and updating your strategy, you can ensure that your investments are aligned with your long-term financial objectives.

In addition to regularly reviewing and assessing your portfolio, it's also important to continue learning and staying informed about the stock market and investing. This may involve reading financial news and analysis, attending educational seminars or workshops, or working with a financial advisor or professional. By staying informed and up-to-date, you can better position yourself for success in the stock market.

Overall, the key to success in the stock market is to have a well-defined investment strategy, regularly review and assess your portfolio, and stay informed and open to new ideas and approaches. By following these principles, you can increase your chances of success as an investor and work towards achieving your financial goals.

Mastering The Art Of Stock Market Investing

www.ingramcontent.com/pod-product-compliance
Lightning Source LLC
Chambersburg PA
CBHW050011230526
45465CB00003BB/1376